Bomber Command Night

Written by Jillian Powell

Contents

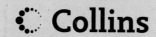

War in Europe

During World War II, Britain and her **allies** fought Germany and her allies. Both sides used bomber and fighter planes.

World War II began in 1939 and ended in 1945.

Bomber Command was part of the Royal Air Force in Britain. Its fleet of bomber planes attacked and destroyed enemy targets on land and at sea.

the **Operations** room of Bomber Command, where night **raids** were planned

Air Chief Marshal Harris led Bomber Command and gave orders for the bombing raids.

Air Chief Marshal Harris

Bomb raids

Many bombing raids were carried out at night. This made it harder for enemy **defences** to spot the bomber planes flying over.

Ground staff at airfields around Britain were told the targets for night raids early in the morning.

Lancaster Bomber

They checked and serviced the bomber planes and filled the fuel tanks.

They towed the bombs to the planes and loaded them into the bomb bays.

They loaded **ammunition** for the guns in the tail **turrets**.

bombs being loaded into the bomb bays

Getting ready

Women's Air Force members packed parachutes for the aircrew.

They checked clothes and **kit** such as goggles, **gas masks** and map bags.

In the kitchens, cooks packed flasks of hot soup or coffee and sandwiches, chocolate and chewing gum for the aircrews.

The briefing

The aircrews were called to the **briefing** room. The commanding officer showed them a map of the target for that night's raid. He gave information about their flight route and times, the weather forecast and enemy defences.

Pilots and navigators used maps to plot their routes to and from the target.

The aircrew

In the crew room, the aircrew put on thick sweaters, flying suits and boots. It was freezing cold on board the bomber planes during night raids.

Flying suits were lined with sheep's wool. Some had electric wires fitted to warm up gloves and boots.

airmen signing for their flying clothes ready for a mission

The airfield

Trucks came to take the aircrews to their planes.

The crews packed their food and kit. Many carried lucky mascots.

Ground staff helped the aircrew get ready for boarding.
They checked clothes, parachutes and map bags.

Take-off

In the tail turrets of the bomber planes, the rear gunners checked their guns.

The aircrews carried out the final checks. The flight engineers signalled they were ready to the ground staff.

The bomber planes taxied to the end of the runway for take-off.

Planes flew together in a **bomber stream** towards the target. This helped them avoid **radar** and searchlights and escape attack by enemy night fighter planes. Often, they were flying so close, there was a risk of crashing in mid-air.

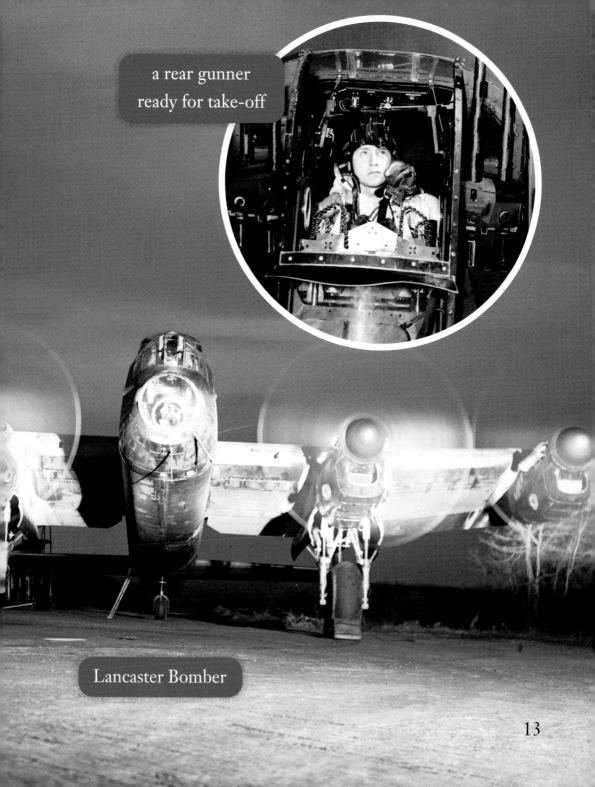

a rear gunner
ready for take-off

Lancaster Bomber

13

The bomb run

Some flights were more than seven hours long. When the bombers reached their target, they began the bomb run.

Radar warned the enemy defences that the bomber planes were coming. They switched on searchlights and fired anti-aircraft guns.

The **bomb aimers** guided the pilots in. They opened the bomb doors and dropped the bombs.

a pilot, navigator and bomb aimer in their positions

Now they had to avoid attack by enemy fighter planes and **flak** from anti-aircraft guns to fly home.

Back home

Ground staff waited nervously for their planes to return. Beacons flashed **Morse code** to guide pilots back to airfields.

Staff cheered when aircrews came into radio contact with the flying control room.

When the planes landed, they helped crews check for flak damage.

aircrew and ground staff looking for flak damage

Aircrews met with an **intelligence officer** to report on the raids.

They sat down to a big breakfast. They could rest until it was time for the next operation.

Remembering Bomber Command

Almost 56,000 Bomber Command aircrew lost their lives in World War II.

Another 10,000 were shot down and captured by the enemy.

Many were in their teens and all were **volunteers**. Some flew up to 80 times, although many were shot down or captured after only a few operations.

the Bomber Command Memorial statue in Green Park, London

THIS MEMORIAL
FROM THE UNITED
& ALLIE
RAF BOMBER C
THE COUR

HM QUEEN ELIZABETH II
UNVEILED THIS MEMORIAL
28 JUNE
IN THE YEAR OF HER DIAMOND JUBILEE
2012

Glossary

allies	countries on the same side in a war
ammunition	things that can be used to attack an enemy such as bombs and bullets
bomb aimers	aircrew who aim bombs at the target
bomber stream	a group of bomber planes flying together
briefing	giving people information about something so they can do their job
defences	people or things that protect something
flak	ammunition fired from guns aimed at enemy aircraft
gas masks	breathing equipment to protect people from poisonous gas
intelligence officer	someone who collects important information after missions
kit	things that may be useful on a trip or job
Morse code	a code based on long and short flashes of light or bleeping noises to show letters of the alphabet
operations	planned missions or jobs
radar	a way of using radio waves to find things that are far away
raids	organised bombing attacks on a place
turrets	posts that hold a gun
volunteers	people who offer to do a job even though they don't have to

Index

A day at Bomber Command

planning the mission

loading the bombs

packing the parachutes

briefing the aircrew

putting on warm clothes

carrying out the mission

having breakfast

23

Ideas for reading

Written by Gillian Howell
Primary Literacy Consultant

Learning objectives: *(reading objectives correspond with Purple band; all other objectives correspond with Diamond band)* read independently and with increasing fluency longer and less familiar texts; understand underlying themes, causes and points of view; improvise using a range of drama strategies and conventions to explore themes such as hopes, fears and desires

Curriculum links: History

Interest words: bomber, fighter, serviced, parachutes, energy, commanding officer, sweaters, engineers, flights, defences, nervously

Resources: whiteboard, pens and paper

Word count: 586

Getting started

- Read the title together and discuss the cover photo with the children. Check that the children understand the context of World War II and that the photograph is of aircrew.

- Turn to the back cover and discuss the blurb together. Ask children what job they think these aircrew had.

- Turn to the contents page. Ask the children to suggest what information each section will give them. Make notes of their suggestions on the whiteboard.

Reading and responding

- Ask the children to read the text aloud quietly. Listen to the children as they read and prompt as needed, e.g. if they read *allies* as *allees*, give them the long *I* sound in the second syllable.

- Remind children to use their phonic knowledge to chop words into chunks of sounds, and then blend the sounds together. Remind them also to look for familiar letter strings to work out words they are unsure of.